Lost Poems of My Youth

Robert O'Brien

Published by Robert O'Brien, 2023.

While every precaution has been taken in the preparation of this book, the publisher assumes no responsibility for errors or omissions, or for damages resulting from the use of the information contained herein.

LOST POEMS OF MY YOUTH

First edition. November 14, 2023.

Copyright © 2023 Robert O'Brien.

ISBN: 979-8223941088

Written by Robert O'Brien.

Foreword

From the time I was seven years old, my world has revolved around baseball. It was more than a sport to me; it was a passion. Playing in the dusty fields, watching games on television, or cheering in the stadium — these were the moments I lived for. I dreamed of nothing else but becoming a baseball player. However, as time passed, it became clear that my skills, while commendable, weren't destined for a professional career. In college, amidst the rigors of finance, accounting, and business studies, I discovered an unexpected refuge in English literature. Elective after elective, my fascination with the world of words grew. It was in these classes that I realized my talent for writing. I began to express myself through poetry, capturing the fleeting images and thoughts that danced in my mind. My creative writing professor, Mr. Cleghorn, once remarked that I possessed a "tender spirit to the world," encouraging me to nurture this gift.

Thus began a journey of words — novels that remained incomplete, songs that echoed the rhythms of my heart, and short stories that spoke of the world as I saw it. It was during this period that I watched "The Rookie," a film starring Dennis Quaid. The story of Jim Morris, a baseball player turned high school coach, resonated deeply with me. His struggle, his reconciliation with an estranged father, and his return to the game he loved — it all mirrored a part of my own life.

One line from the movie struck a chord: "It's alright to think about what you want to do until it's time to start doing what you were meant to do." I had always believed I was meant for baseball, but life had other plans. Had I pursued that single dream, I would have missed out on the joys of my present — a loving wife, children, stepsons, grandchildren, and my faithful dogs.

I now understand that I was always meant to be a writer. It is through writing that I share the tapestry of my dreams, memories, and fantasies. This book is a testament to that journey — an unedited collection spanning my formative years in high school to the threshold of adulthood, where the realities of life momentarily dimmed my passion for writing.

In these pages, I invite you to partake in the journey of a dreamer who found his true calling in the magic of words.

Poems

I Remember

I remember.
How we walked
On the mountainside
I see your face.
Standing by the river
In the still of night
The fish swim upstream.
Back to life
I hoped to see.
But never found.
A trace of you
I look back.
The cries of happiness
Canoeing in the river
I feel your stroke.
I see your love for nature.
I feel your emotion.
I see your image.
And devotion
I feel your thoughts.
And I understand.

Daddy

A door buzzes open in a crowded cell block.
Disturbed faces peer outward in hope
The guards escort the convict like a movie star.
On his way to a theater's final show
The stage a table with no curtains to close
The setting a clean room with a wide window
The audience, the family and those who chose.
To see a play with no crescendo
Restless children do not understand.
The lost reality, the justice of man
He lay on the table, his arm full of pain.
Daddy is gone for he died in vain.

Castle

The starving knight
Hacked away the vines.
And killed the moat monster.
To reach the castle
And open the door.
To Grandma's house.

No Ones Cottage on the Shore

There's a cottage on the shore where no one lives.
Along a beach where no one walks.
There is a wooden door with no ones locks.
And a telephone where no one talks.
In the cottage where no one lives.
There is a chair at the table where no one eats.
And a place on the couch where no one sits.
There's a book on the table that no one reads.
A lamp on the wall that no one lit,
A blanket in the corner that no one warms.
And a fireplace in the corner that no one lights
There's a cup in the kitchen that no one fills.
An apron on the wall that no one wears.
A pot in the cupboard that no one heats.
Food in the pantry that no one eats.
There's a pillow on the bed where no one lies.
A rack in the closet with no one's clothes
A toothbrush in the bathroom for no one's teeth
And slippers on the floor for no one's feet
I wish no one was home everyday.
For now, she has chosen to stay away.

I was a Pepperoni Pizza

I was a pepperoni pizza.
Beat and punched until flat.
Then splatted with gew and icky green stuff.
Oh, the massage of hands.
The chorus of olives and onions
The smothering grip of mozzarella
Then off to the oven for a steam bath
Waiting, waiting, to the table I go
The confusion of hands after the biggest
Slice of my hot body
The symphony of teeth and tongue
Grinding, crushing until washed down.
With a cold Miller Lite
Stop, I can't take it.
Spit me back up.
Then the slosh of a wet slimy mop

Challenger

It was on a February morning.
when the engines fired like pandemonium
And the seven boarded its outspread wings.
while the cold wind reaped of
foreboding doom.
Above the ground a bright omniscient glow
Scattered chaos and debris into the air
Sighs and horror filled the faces below.
People torn with perpetual despair.
All the kings' horses couldn't make it right.
A nation struck into a state of mourn.
Fingers of blame pointing at those of might.
Their lives, the seven would God adorn.
To begin again is man's destiny.
Will last all through eternity.

A Poetic Translation of
A Revelation to John

People are flashing out of place.
A new beginning for the human race
A new thing exciting to see.
A bright new city above the sea
The prophet kneeled.
Before a bright glowing light
A figure who told him
To sit down and write
In the image of Jesus
Called Son of Man
Wearing a long robe
with a bright golden band
Seven stars in his palm
And a sword for a tongue
His face like the sun
His hair white as wool
His voice to seven candles
Seven churches of old
"These things I will show you.
To them must be told"
How candles will burn
By the light of a fire
Enough to incite desire.

A gathering earth
The spirit of the lord
Seated among 24 elders in gold crowns.
Four beasts sat like pets.
And all before him fell down.
*A book with seven seals
The lamb opened one.
A sound of great thunder
The four beasts said, "Come."
And the horses came.
Each a different shade
White, red, and black
And then one of jade
Their riders brought destruction.
Famine and disease
The stars fell from the sky.
Like figs from their trees
The sun a fiery red
Like cans in a drunkard's nook
The moon became as blood.
And all men hid in the rocks.
The trumpets blew.
Each a different wrath
The water turned poison.
The earth a blood bath
Locust went to battle.
Dressed in armor of iron.
Breathing fire and smoke
With the roar of a lion
Then the mighty angel told
The prophet to eat.
The scroll of the angel

So sour, so sweet
The seventh trumpet blew.
And the elders said.
"Lord God Almighty,
Time to judge the dead."
Then came the beast of the earth.
And the beast of the sea.
Writing the number on the foreheads
Of the ones it deceived
And the angel with seven plagues
Killed all in the sea.
Dried up great Euphrates.
Burned with fierce heat.
Babylon fell.
Great quake and fire
With hail and millstone
A great funeral pyre
A white horse appeared.
"Faithful and True" his name
The rider covered with blood.
His eyes like a flame
The armies of heaven
Followed him on white steeds.
To do battle with Satan
And all souls to free
Then came a great feast.
As the beast was retired
His sentence to be thrown.
Into the Lake of Fire
Satan was defeated.
And so, his empire
After 1000 years loused

Thrown in the lake of fire.
On judgement day
The book of life
If ones name not appeared
"Cast into the lake of fire.
The sea, death, and hell
Give up it's dead.
Cast into the Lake of fire.
Those would be judged again.
Then a new heaven
A bright new city of precious stone
The throne of God
And the promise it shown.
Of Jesus's return
To New Jerusalem he'll come
As a "bright morning star"
A Revelation to John

Shopping Malls

Shopping malls and shopping stalls
Women off to the races
Board men ponder the wide world of Sports.
Overburdened with packages full of things not for them.
A secret conspiracy, CHARGE say the women.
I've only 50 pairs of shoes!
End of month bills, end of month thrills
Cutting up charge cards
Watching the women weep like wounded cats.
But I need more clothes the women implore,
Honey you're not Emelda Marcos
So shut up and eat your dinner!

Icicles and Poppy Seeds

The sun sets early today in the trees.
And the animals go home for a sleep.
The only sound is the familiar bleat.
Of the moon under the night's canopy.
Wind like icicles kisses barren knees.
Of saplings wrapped in an armor like sheath
The hunter's pipe blows a white ghastly wreath.
While his body is warmed with pungent tea
The night is cold but warming to him.
The trees stretch from a must slumbering peace.
And hold their hands to the sun once again.
Off in the distance a bird's song is heard.
The hunter drives off to his city hearth.
And the forest has kept its golden fleece.

Cat

Put sat out did the cat.
And chased the cat did the rat.
So, rat said the drat.
For the trap set the cat
But the fat was too rat.
So, the zap he did rat.
And he mat on the sat.
The nap took a cat.
And the pat did brat.
The mat on the cat
On his cat put the lap
His wrap did he cat.
And that was all that.
The day did all cat.

Challenger

It was on a February morning.
when the engines fired like pandemonium
And the seven boarded it's outspread wings.
while the cold wind reaped of
foreboding doom.
Above the ground a bright omniscient glow
Scattered chaos and debris into the air
Sighs and horror filled the faces below.
People torn with perpetual despair.
All the kings' horses couldn't make it right.
A nation struck into a state of mourn.
Fingers of blame pointing at those of might.
Their lives, the seven would God adorn.
To begin again is man's destiny.
Will last all through eternity.

Prayer

Keep safe the sunrise.
The innocence of the morning
For those whose lives are incomplete
Let the evening rain.
Break the mountain's silence.
And color their forest green
Hold those hands that clutch.
Cane and wheel
Deliver them into peace.
Let them walk through golden sand.
On heaven's beach
Give food and drink.
To burning stomachs.
Let live the tiny child.
Let them taste the joy of apple trees.
Fill little faces with smiles.
Care for those whose thoughts are lost.
Locked away in a room.
Help gentle winds clear their opaque sky.
Turn darkness into light.
Let blind eyes see wild open meadows.
And silent ears hear trickling brook.
Help straining lips sing words of love.
Songs of a deer's steady look
Kiss the withered faces,

Whose candles burned so long.
Let them sleep under a strong oak tree.
And play on heaven's lawn.
Keep safe the sunrise.

Grandpa

Grandpa is in the hospital.
I don't know why.
Grandma says it's cancer.
But grandpas aren't supposed to die.
She said Jesus came down from heaven.
And took my grandpa away.
He left us all alone.
To live another day
Are you okay Grandpa,
Can you hear me now?
Are you in that cloud?
Grandpa, please come down",
I know now you have died.
Some day we can play.
When Jesus comes for me
And takes me too away.

Crystal Oasis

In the forest and bosky shadows
A cold magical river gleams like wax
It's water the color of emerald moon beams.
Reflect off a sheer crystal bank.
The other bank a slow rising mountain
Curtains this solemn Eden
Sweat from last year's snow trickles,
Down to the trepid current
Walking by the river, the years
As recent as yesterday, flashed through my mind.
Looking at the bottom of the waterfall
The maelstrom of moral conflict
A deer drinks from the pool it forms.
I climbed that lighted crystal bank.
Figures of phantasm from a crystal ball
I reached for them but fell,
Into the icy pit of the river.
It' dagger pierced my mind.
Nature has always been so kind.
The tears of God strewn across the night sky.
Cried over the hum of chainsaws,
The drumfire of bombs and guns.
Sitting by the pool in the arrest of night,
The passion of the campfire warms me.
And I cry, for tomorrow I dream again.

Ever More A Part

The president and all the aces
Must walk a different march.
And build a new morality,
Ever more a part.
The joker must not attend.
It must be from the heart.
To mold a new destiny,
Ever more a part.
To triumph the hand of God,
Is to play the losing card.
Will last all through eternity,
Ever more a part.
To fold our hand to Jesus,
Is the way to play it smart.
And grow into his quality,
Ever more a part.

Endless Highway

Another day goes by
Without a sound
Caught up inside the traffic.
Of the human mind
We try to hide our thoughts.
Underneath the ground
Visions of a fantasy world
A world without no end
One with endless highways
An exit for every sin
We try to shut out reality.
We try to keep it in
Trapped inside a box.
With no way out
It's getting smaller each day.
With every waking hour
We try to hold it back.
Before its final collapse
It's like we're on a train,
With no bound destiny
Running on the railroad tracks
Of a dying world
We try to jump off,
Only to board again
Wake me before I go,

Because I may never wake
Dying on thoughts of tomorrow
Of all our mistakes
Wake me before I go,
To that fantasy place
Sleeping in endless slumber
Never again to see your face

A Picture of Me

Across a crowded room she stands,
Staring like an avid fan,
At a picture of me on the wall,
When I was too young to learn to crawl.
She asks me who that boy might be,
And I say to her that it was me,
In a time when nations clashed at war,
And people were dying score by score.
I told her I was too young to see,
The millions of children just like me,
Dying in battles they never won,
Crying to see if help would come.
Lastly, I told her I hung it there,
To remember there's a time when all should be scared.

Houston

Close your eyes,
Unto the night
A city solemnly sleeps.
No traffic cops,
No traffic stops,
The streets dark and empty.
Where have all the people gone?
The life of the city,
They have gone to their homes,
In another city.
What traitors we are,
To live so far,
From the source of our wealth.
A city dies,
It cannot hide,
The state of its health.
Move to the city,
Don't stray from its center,
Hold your velocity.
Grow like L.A.,
Stand broad like Chicago,
Look tall like New York,
Have no civilian embargo.
And greatness will come,
And live in the streets,

Unto the night,
A city solemnly sleeps.

A Captain's Song

I'm all screwed up,
My life is not my own.
I feel the forces pulling on me,
Tearing pieces of me away,
Leaving me with nothing,
Nothing but pain.
Like a tug of war rope,
Both ends taunt,
Coming unraveled, soon to break.
And then nothing more.
The ship I am on,
Driven into the reef,
Sinking beneath my feet.
Then I'm tied to the wheel,
The constant bombardment,
Of the forces,
Seeking to control me.
I will not give in,
They will not succeed.
In the end I'll go down,
Captain of my ship.
Driven to insanity,
By those who control me.
No rope to pull me in,
To save me from my destiny.

Only hope that I'll give in,
Hope that they'll control me.
No kind heart to rescue me,
And shield me from the war.
Comfort I shall never know.
Until I am no more.

Honor in Grace

Great frontier
Oh, how we cheer,
Each step that we take.
In greatness and in fear
Into space we do peer
To explore for other race
Devoted pride
God will provide.
Journey into space
The seven departed
Across the sky
Only to find
Plans gone awry.
No one to blame.
The shuttle to flame
The rain of innocent sky
A country wept.
God will protect,
Those who believe in him.
The few that we mourn,
To him they are born,
In his grace we say goodbye.
The strength of men,
To begin again,
The destiny of his race.

Remember of well,
Those whom I tell,
Who died in the name of space.

The Last to Remember

The last to remember,
Are the chosen few.
Who survived the world,
Who will start all new.
Will history repeat,
Will man defeat,
His love for life.
The war is over,
The few are free,
To live all alone,
In their iniquity.
Divided by past,
Or history,
The living live,
The dead are free.
Insanity prevails,
Across the sky,
The sun is dark,
The land is dry.
The living are scarce,
Spread over time,
Memories remind,
Of yesterday.
Only a few,
Can forget the past,

To begin again,
To make it all last.
To remember back,
Across the mind,
The terrible war,
Peace for mankind.

Big Men

Big men with big plans,
Gathered from two opposite lands.
To a point of neutrality,
A summit of reality.
The streets of Geneva,
Reflect the feeling,
The distrust among men,
The way its always been.
Big men with big dreams,
No not what each mean,
When they talk of a hate,
With a terrible fate.
Who will concede,
Who will give up,
Can there be trust,
Without atomic lust.
The world stands still,
With these men on a hill,
Watching with bright eyes.
Who lives and who dies.
How long can two men,
Stand before a crowd,
Before they become friends,
Before it all ends.
Big men rock the world,

With funnels in the sky,
Shadows racing overhead,
Deciding who will die.
Sleep is impossible,
Sleep will never come,
Until the world is at peace,
Before big men are done.

Visiting Light

Visiting light,
You've invaded my night,
My inner thoughts concede.
The world awaits,
Your lonely fate,
So let me not impede.
Through asteroid belt,
And spacey velvet,
Your course doth you speed.
In the quiet night,
Of heavens light,
The legends that you breed.
Neptune's tune,
Of forgotten moons,
The colors that Saturn bleeds.
We trust your light,
As a common sight,
To look in skyward need.

Exit of Man

Live, before you die,
The wasteland is long and dry.
Go, before you fall,
Into the abyss of mortal life.
Running in circles,
The monotony of the street,
The sound you can't hear,
Disturbs the mind.
The wishing well,
Of a new religion,
Is full of lies,
Of hollow meaning.
Look for the oasis,
A gap in the desert,
Drink the water of life,
And exit this land.
Live among living,
Not speaking of dreams,
Hold on to reality,
Know what it means.
When the time has come,
Look to the sky,
The home of the Gods,
The dreams don't lie.
Your life eclipsed,

The time is near,
Travel to the abyss,
The sound you can't hear.

Souls

Oh, gentle rain,
On desperate sky,
Hear this wish,
I make tonight.
Bring to me,
That which is lost,
Search in the desert,
Search in the frost.
Lost is my soul,
In direction know not,
Without it I'll die,
Just sit here and rot.
It gives me hope,
Strength and desire,
It is the spark,
That sends my heart fire.
It is my mind,
Conscience and friend,
It supposed to stay,
With me to the end.
I like other men,
Have seen it escape,
In my mind I see,
It murder and rape.
Of the knowledge of life,

I sit here and write,
Come back to my body,
Come back tonight.

Tentative Thoughts

Tentative thoughts of forgotten love,
Never ever remembered of.
Who could ever face this feat,
And explain a language we often speak.
Repeated over eons of time,
In some tongue or frame of mind.
Which relates to us the things we need,
And has become our unlearned creed.
Stating simply that life goes on,
Despite what many things go wrong,
It binds our thoughts of trust and love,
And has become our ticket to the world above.

Wind

Blow oh wind from the northern sky,
So cold, so frigid, so hard, so dry,
That makes the leaves fall from their trees,
That keeps the river from the sea.
Blow oh wind, what is your tale,
That makes my flesh look so pale.
Are you telling me something that isn't true,
Or are you just being you?
Wind oh wind I see your fate,
You're just the object of my cold hate.
You cool the earth and strip the trees,
And do the things God wished thy to be.

To The Secretary

I sit in an office,
Hot and Humid,
Heavy with the scent of cigarette smoke
I hear the ticking, clicking, clatter of the typewriter,
And the dull roar of the Xerox machine.
My body tired from people pushing me,
All day long.
My boss covers me with paperwork,
Endless stacks of numbers to be counted.
I count numbers,
Juggling them in an office circus.
Counting, sorting, adding, carry the one,
Divide, subtract, multiply, remember,
I count all day long.
Turning numbers into accounting information
The hours drag along while,
Work in the office hurries
I run from desk to desk,
Finishing unfinished piles of work
People spilling coffee on me,
And yelling at me because my
Answer isn't right.
My work spills onto the floor
Piled up like ticker tape,
I am so busy,

44

No time to break for lunch.
I become tired,
In need of rest.
As the office closes,
I go home to a dark room,
Where I sleep until tomorrow.

Common Entity

Alone tonight, I sit in fright,
Afraid for the human race
For it is from this fear, That I cry a tear,
For those who died in space
An endless dream, A sparkled stream,
Flowing throughout infinity.
A record of time, That astounds the mind,
The picture of a galaxy.
Every falling star, Every burning sun,
Every comet that I see.
Burns in my heart, A desiring part,
To explore my curiosity.
For only the stars, Caused man to spar,
With his own destiny.
His progress is seen, In the things that he brings,
Into the galaxy.
A voyager greets, Each planet it meets,
With a voice of hospitality.
His picture he sends, Surprises all men,
Projecting reality.
The milk of the heaven, And the death of the seven
Shared a common entity.

Winter

It comes,
Like a church mouse.
Gnawing, clawing,
At the shingles on my house.
Then it grows fierce,
Like a Tiger's rage.
Stripping the trees,
Blowing the leaves.
Its breath is so cold.
Then, it snows,
For four long months.
It stands on the ground,
Beating the grass down,
Biting the pale flesh
Of the earth.
Hush, Hush,
The first Robin appears,
Landing in the naked tree,
It's a song that I hear.
So long, So long,
It's time to say goodbye.
Then the snow melts,
And the cold wind dies,
The leaves return,
And the grasses rise.

April is here,
The cruelest month of all.
The Tiger sleeps,
Until next fall.

The Bag Lady

I saw the old bag lady,
In the alley today.
Her feeble leather hands pushing
A cart with creaky squeaky wheels.
Scaring the rats in the alley
Into the twilight.
She looked like an old alley cat,
Searching the trash cans for
Morsels to survive on.
Her clothes were tattered and torn,
And layered upon her body like earth.
Her hair and skin were
Darkened like stained wood with dirt.
Her face faceless
An Egyptian Sphinx
Weathered with the years.
Her eyes still, like pieces of coal
Once burned to a tear.
She walks hunched over,
And with a limp,
Because a mugger knocked her down.
Every day she journeys to the park,
To share what little she has
With the pigeons.
No one talks to her,

No one stops.
"Go on, move along!" says the cop.
No friends but pigeons,
So lonely, her life,
She walks back to the alley,
Under the tears of night,
To find a warm place to rest.
She sleeps in a trash pile,
Her blanket a newspaper
Reading, "Coldest Winter Yet."
Her pillow her bag
Laced with old shoestrings,
Weary of its age.
She dreams of nothing,
For her dreams have all gone,
But tomorrow's sorrow,
Dawn.

Flash

Flash, a bright glowing red,
A mushroom cloud dead ahead.
Rising to the heavens afar,
Knocking this great world ajar.
Flash, people crying in vain,
Don't have a chance to feel the pain.
Falling by thousands to the dust,
Pictures of a dying trust.
Flash, our world is no more,
For there is no ending final score.
But if a score there must be,
Strike one under for the land of the free.

Quest

The kings' men ride,
All through the night.
Their quest in essence unreal.
To search for something,
They cannot see,
Hear, smell, or feel.
The truth of life,
The key to the door,
A search for reality,
A chance to explore.
The chambers of the mind,
Filled with endless hallways,
But we find ourselves,
Up against the wall.
Trapped by our conscience,
We try to think,
Why our lives,
Have a missing link.
That without this part,
We are not whole,
Our lives as meaningless,
As an empty bowl.
We are the kings' men,
In search for purpose,
We live by the rule,

That others put on us.
If we try to escape,
We cannot hide,
The barriers we built,
Are as strong as our pride.
To let go from reality,
Is freedom and hope,
A chance to relieve,
The tension of our rope.
And someday soon,
When we find the key,
We'll realize how little,
We think of thee.

A Chickadee's Nightmare

A melodious chickadee sinks in the plush snow's peace,
That unrolls like a scroll on the earth.
Above in a gondola, unsheathed from its home,
A lazy hippopotamus is eating a pristine pickle.
Thinking of a tranquil elegant ride,
The reek of his breath and his crooked stomachache,
Discombobulates an assuaging ride.
The gondola falls and the chickadee escapes the hippo's pale flesh.

Prophecy

Rolling are the mountains,
Towering to the skies.
Rushing are the rivers,
Running to the sea.
If God had wanted war,
These would never have been meant to be.

A Picture of Me

Across a crowded room she stands,
Staring like an avid fan,
At a picture of me on the wall,
When I was too young to learn to crawl.
She asks me who that boy might be,
And I say to her that it was me,
In a time when nations clashed at war,
And people were dying score by score.
I told her I was too young to see,
The millions of children just like me,
Dying in battles they never won,
Crying to see if help would come.
Lastly, I told her I hung it there,
To remember there's a time when all should be scared.

Tentative Thoughts

Tentative thoughts of forgotten love,
Never ever remembered of.
Who could ever face this feat,
And explain a language we often speak.
Repeated over eons of time,
In some tongue or frame of mind.
Which relates to us the things we need,
And has become our unlearned creed.
Stating simply that life goes on,
Despite what many things go wrong,
It binds our thoughts of trust and love,
And has become our ticket to the world above.

Wind

Blow oh wind from the northern sky,
So cold, so frigid, so hard, so dry,
That makes the leaves fall from their trees,
That keeps the river from the sea.
Blow oh wind, what is your tale,
That makes my flesh look so pale.
Are you telling me something that isn't true,
Or are you just being you.
Wind oh wind I see your fate,
You're just the object of my cold hate.
You cool the earth and strip the trees,
And do the things God wished thy to be.

A CONNOTATION OF GRIEF

Canto 1

A force from outside my head
Invades my inner thoughts.
To control my every move
As if watching with seerful eyes
The old man kneels and cries.
'How can this be?
That there is no sea,
No coral, no fish, no reed,
No ground for this ships need.'
He stops to think and see,
His face aging in the mirror
As if his purpose has ceased,
The sea has surrendered.
Man brings about change,
Corrupts all of life,
Building here and building there,
Hushing nature's musical fife.
Man plays a different tune,
Bass, no treble exists,
To brighten its sound.
Only bass, only death
In this land can be found.
Painful to ears I hear,
Mournful tunes of lamentation

59

Over the hollow lives
Ended by jovial activities,
Where liaison affairs engage,
Interrupting the social course of the evening.
Yet I wonder in thought,
To the whimsical world
The exit of mankind
"Not with a bang, but a whimper."

Canto 2

A distant sky
Crawls up from the horizon
Flashing lights disturb the air,
Around which we breathe.
This ship I am on
Draws near to the edge,
Teetering over reality
The fallacy of all men
The way it has always been.
The sound grows stronger,
Deafening to the ears.
The cries of humanity,
The work of insanity,
Breaking off pieces of the world,
Feeding them to the fire,
Warming our desire
To continue the destruction
Of the human mind.
Only, the fire grows bigger,
Engulfing the insanity,
Steering this ship
Into the fire of greed.

Giving up when there is no need.

Canto 3

Oh, let me hear,
The sound of cheer,
The clap of an audience
Listening to the joys of today.
The women at play,
The world is afraid,
And time stands still.
Thinking in circles
Of how it would be
To have no light,
Just ash and dust our lungs to breathe.
No city lights,
Just torch and flame,
Burning the diseased
When there is no need.
Irony tells, man expels,
The destiny of his race.
Cash in your chips
Before you lose.
Walk away ahead,
Bet once more,
The odds will score,
Our world will be no more.

Canto 4

A cold sensation,
The rising of the moon,
The tears of innocent night,
Wish I may or might.
The destiny of man,
Acquitted by insanity,
Rebuilt under nightfall,

In the homes of innocent land.
The fallacy of complete,
Yet time commands our feet,
To move in forward progress,
To still another defeat.
The washing of the hands
Cleanses our soul,
Bearing gifts to our God,
Repeating time has told.
Where is the hand,
That commands the land.
To strive, succeed, defy,
Is it raised in anger,
Or hid in idle fear.
The faith of the mighty yield
In fortress and in field
The battles done forbade,
Our anger that we trade,
The tears of innocent night

Canto 5

Portrait of reality
A summit of neutrality,
The distrust among men,
The way it's always been.
In arms negotiation,
Two facial expressions
Afraid to speak their peace,
To give up their golden fleece.
For the future of man,
Depends on a plan,
To bring to an end
The weapons they defend.

Before smiles become frowns,
Before cities become ground.
How long can two men,
Sit at opposite ends,
Looking distraught,
With fingers taunt,
Over weapons of hate.
Before it's too late,
In the future I see,
These two become three,
Then four and five,
And twenty-four and twenty-five.

Canto 6

Every time the sun sets
A part of me fades away.
Like the image of my shadow
When I step into the shade.
Follow the path of light,
That weaves among the trees.
Do not stray away,
For your shadow you won't see.
When the night comes,
Stay near the open flame,
If it goes out,
You've only yourself to blame.
Wake with the morning dew,
Complete the walk of life.
When you reach the end
God will ease your strife.
Live among the heavens
Where there is no shade,

Just the beauty of the universe,
And the glory of the day.

Canto 7

Across the golden meadow
Underneath an opaque sky,
The cattle graze in immunity
From the diseased world outside.
I hop the laser fence,
And through the meadow I fly,
In the direction of the cattle,
Food for a hungry tribe.
A warrior steps across me,
And looks me in the eyes,
He sees the hunger in my face,
But fails to let me by.
He says the cattle graze,
On meadow, grass, and maze,
Not for the outside world,
But for the heads of state.
I turn in retreat,
Listening to his news,
The sympathy of the government
No longer includes me and you.
Returning to my tribe,
With extended empty hands,
They frown, cry, and die,
Across a desperate land.

Canto 8

Feelings riding on a crowded bus,
Dreams distorted by light.
As we journey to the city,
Can we make it right?
Change the illusion of life,
Like a changing traffic light.
Though thoughts betray our motives,
Hidden from our sight,
Soon the door will open.
The hearts of men escape,
The power turns to overrule,
Rhythms turn to shape.
Images and formless design
Break in the prism frame,
Answers turn to questions,
An everlasting endless game.
No center is contrived,
Like ripples in the sea,
A canopy of stars,
Will feed this burning need.
Feel the push of raindrops,
In the wishing well of hope.
Capture signs of grand design,
Discover as thoughts elope.
Compress the future in your fist,
Feel its mighty bruise,
Let go the reign of eternity,
Itself in end will lose.

Canto 9

Understanding,
Is the question of dreams.
A visual collage,
Of past and present scenes.
Biorhythms pulse with energy,
Collected in our thoughts,
Emitted as static dreams,
We must connect the dots.
Piecing a shattered illusion,
Together in a frame,
An answer to the question,
Born without a name.
A picture of a human thought,
A best laid scheme,
Protected by our ignorance,
Of its underlying theme.
Its meaning a fracture,
In the cord of reverie,
Must connect the thread,
Unlock our pillory.
how our insecure spots,
A target for deadly sin,
Must dodge the blade of suicide,
Must hold our feelings in.

Canto 10

The day is hot,
The runway is dry.
A lone plane sits,
To live or to die.
I see faces of uncertainty,
Prayer and strife,
Held hostage by gunmen,
In fear of their life.
What possessed these men,
To go so wrong,
To free their own kind,
A cause they can't find.
Why do they kill,
And whose blood do they spill,
Those who need not,
Those who got caught.
In the middle of insanity,
From demented minds.
Plans that unravel,
Peace of mankind.
How often we wonder,
What pushes these men,
To take their own lives,
For the purpose of sin.
To the terrorist I say,
Be gone and away,
Cross over to death,
Take your last breath.

Canto 11

Age is in the mind,
Youth is in the body,
As they go their separate ways.
What shall we do next?
One runs out the other,
An incomplete cycle,
One forgets the other,
A reversed cycle.
Time controls both,
Pulling them along,
As the years go by,
Which will die first?
The mind or the body,
Linked only in space,
Confined in reality,
A thought for every place.
If the mind goes first,
We become extinct abstract.
If the body goes first,
We become extinct.
There must be a reason,
An answer to our question.
What happens to us when we die?
There must be a third,
Not controlled by time,
The soul is ourself,
Both body and mind.
With or without it,
We eventually die,
Is the form,
We take in the sky.

Canto 12

I see a village,
But no people.
A train and
No rider.
A playground,
Without children.
A car with
No driver.
I see many stones,
On which history tells,
The ones who died,
And now here they do dwell.
Many together
In graves they do lay,
Buried together,
In the haste of the day.
When man killed himself,
The innocent ones,
All life now has ended,
And nobody won .
What we all feared
Has finally come,
No one could stop it,
Until it was done.

Canto 13

A white powder
Controls the mind,
Like Kubla Khan
And the Rime.
A "pleasure dome",
For the thoughts of men.
With the trip back,
A desperate plan,
A hunt for the demon,
On the streets of town.
Through back alley and stairway,
Search for the gown.
Of death and enchantment,
Eliot's Hollow men,
Wandering on the banks,
A river and no end.
This mighty substance,
Hunts and destroys,
Men submerged in suggestion,
It's deadly ploy.
To drain all of life,
From the caverns of the mind,
To build its walls and towers,
Around those who it finds.
Its assertion is evil,
Its asset is man,
Its goal is to kill,
Where the river ran.

About the Author

Robert M. O'Brien is a seasoned Data & AI Associate Director with an esteemed career in a large consulting firm in the Houston area, Texas. Drawing from his extensive expertise in technology, Robert has published numerous studies and documents that have made significant contributions to the field of IT Consulting and Advanced Analytics. A man of diverse talents, who has traveled the world, he has also ventured into the realm of literature with his self-published book, "We Were Boys," a unique collection that captures real events of teenage boys through the lens of imagination. Robert aspires to devote his time to full-time writing and his current projects, weaving more intricate narratives and engaging tales that resonate with readers and expand his literary repertoire and further explore the realms of historical fiction, dystopian narratives, and beyond.

Read more at www.booksbyrobertobrien.com.

Milton Keynes UK
Ingram Content Group UK Ltd.
UKHW020944221123
433051UK00020B/958

9 798223 941088